Milton Hershey
and the Chocolate Industry

Katie Kawa

PowerKiDS
press.

New York

Published in 2017 by The Rosen Publishing Group, Inc.
29 East 21st Street, New York, NY 10010

First Edition

Editor: Sarah Machajewski
Book Design: Mickey Harmon

Photo Credits: Cover, pp. 1–8, 10, 12–26, 28, 30–32 (series design) Melodist/Shutterstock.com; cover, p. 1 (Milton Hershey), p. 24 (Katherine Hershey) ASSOCIATED PRESS/APImages.com; p. 5 Scott Olson/Staff/Getty Images News/Getty Images; p. 7 Education Images/UIG/Getty Images; p. 9 Shaiith/Shutterstock.com; p. 11 nano/Getty Images; p. 13 Lissandra Melo/Shutterstock.com; p. 14 AlenKadr/Shutterstock.com; p. 15 (inset) Rick Sause Photography/Shutterstock.com; p. 15 (kisses) Bloomberg/Contributor/Bloomberg/Getty Images; p. 17 https://en.wikipedia.org/wiki/Derry,_Pennsylvania#/media/File:Derry_Station_PA_1900_BEye_View.jpg; p. 19 Culture Club/Contributor/Hulton Archive/Getty Images; pp. 21, 29 George Sheldon/Shutterstock.com; p. 22 Lissandra Melo/Shutterstock.com; p. 23 karenfoleyphotography/Shutterstock.com; p. 25 Underwood Archives/Contributor/Getty Images; p. 26 Sheila Fitzgerald/Shutterstock.com; p. 27 Michael G McKinne/Shutterstock.com.

Library of Congress Cataloging-in-Publication Data

Names: Kawa, Katie, author.
Title: Milton Hershey and the chocolate industry / Katie Kawa.
Description: New York : PowerKids Press, [2017] | Series: Great entrepreneurs in U.S. history | Includes index.
Identifiers: LCCN 2016016332 | ISBN 9781499421354 (paperback) | ISBN 9781499421378 (library bound) | ISBN 9781499421361 (6 pack)
Subjects: LCSH: Hershey, Milton Snavely, 1857-1945–Juvenile literature. | Businessmen–United States–Biography–Juvenile literature. | Chocolate industry–United States–History–Juvenile literature. | Hershey Foods Corporation–History–Juvenile literature. | Hershey (Pa.)–Biography–Juvenile literature. | Hershey (Pa.)–Economic conditions–Juvenile literature.
Classification: LCC HD9200.U52 H474 2017 | DDC 338.7/66392092 [B] –dc23
LC record available at https://lccn.loc.gov/2016016332

Manufactured in the United States of America

CPSIA Compliance Information: Batch #BS16PK: For Further Information contact Rosen Publishing, New York, New York at 1-800-237-9932

Contents

A Sweet Story

Today, it's easy to go into a store and buy a chocolate bar without spending a lot of money. However, that wasn't always true. In the past, chocolate was a treat only wealthy people could afford. That changed around the turn of the 20th century, with an American entrepreneur, or businessman, named Milton Hershey. He led this revolution in the chocolate industry.

Hershey took the principles of mass production that were a major part of the Industrial Revolution and applied them to the process of making milk chocolate. In doing so, he made chocolate that was affordable for the average American. Hershey was known as a great entrepreneur. He was also known as a man who used his success to help others. Now *that's* a sweet story!

Chocolate: An American Treat

Milton Hershey didn't invent chocolate. In fact, by the time he was born, chocolate had already been eaten as a treat for hundreds of years. Chocolate is made using beans from the cacao plant, which is native to the Americas. Cacao beans, which are also called cocoa beans, were first used by ancient Native American peoples, including the Maya and Aztecs. They used these beans to make a drink for members of the upper class. This chocolate drink was then brought back to Europe by explorers who'd traveled to the Western Hemisphere.

Milton Hershey is best known for being the first American to mass-produce milk chocolate. Today, "Hershey" is still the most famous name in the American chocolate industry!

Growing Up in Pennsylvania

Milton Snavely Hershey was born on September 13, 1857. His parents—Henry Hershey and Veronica "Fanny" Snavely Hershey—were two very different people. His mother was a practical woman who believed in working hard. His father was a dreamer who couldn't make his dreams a reality. Hershey watched his father fail many times as a businessman, which surely made him work even harder to succeed.

Hershey was born in Derry Township, Pennsylvania. At this time, this part of central Pennsylvania was mainly farmland. Hershey didn't receive much of an education. Once he became successful, he wanted to help young people get a better education than he had growing up. In 1909, he started a school to help children in need get the best education possible.

Hershey traveled away from Derry Township as he grew up. He returned there to build a chocolate factory in 1903. The community of Hershey, Pennsylvania, grew around that factory, turning Hershey's birthplace into what's now called "The Sweetest Place on Earth."

Hershey Keeps Trying

When Hershey was a teenager, he began working as an apprentice in Lancaster, Pennsylvania. An apprentice is a person who learns a job by working for someone who is already skilled in that job. At first, he worked as a printer's apprentice, but he wasn't good at that kind of trade. Then, he began working as an apprentice for a confectioner, or a person who makes candy and other sweets.

Hershey discovered he had a talent for making candy, and he liked this kind of work. In 1876, he traveled to Philadelphia to start his own candy business. That business failed, but Hershey didn't give up. He traveled to many cities, including Denver, Colorado, to learn more. He opened a new business in New York City, but this business also failed. In 1886, he returned to Pennsylvania after losing all his money in his failed candy businesses.

Although Hershey's early candy businesses didn't succeed, he didn't stop trying. He learned important things from his failures that helped him later in his career.

The Lancaster Caramel Company

When Hershey returned to Pennsylvania, he tried once again to start a candy-making business. He wanted to make caramels using fresh milk, which was a method he learned in Denver. Hershey started this new business in the town of Lancaster.

Unlike Hershey's other businesses, the Lancaster Caramel Company became a success. A British candy seller placed a large order for Hershey's caramels, and that order allowed him to grow his business in a way he couldn't before. Soon, he had 1,400 employees and his products were shipped around the United States and the world.

The success of the Lancaster Caramel Company showed Hershey that people liked candy made with fresh milk. This would be very important a few years later, when Hershey began developing his most famous contribution to the candy industry.

The Lancaster Candy Company made Hershey a millionaire! He sold the company in August 1900 for $1 million. He then focused on making chocolates instead of caramels.

From Caramels to Chocolates

In 1893, Hershey visited Chicago, Illinois, during the World's Columbian Exposition, or World's Fair. During this visit, he saw a German exhibit about the process of making chocolate. It inspired Hershey to make his own chocolate. He bought all the equipment in the exhibit to use in his caramel factory.

At first, Hershey only made chocolate coatings and flavorings for his caramels, but he soon came to believe that chocolates would sell better than caramels. In 1894, he established the Hershey Chocolate Company. Hershey was soon making 114 **varieties** of chocolate.

The Hershey Chocolate Company made sweet chocolate, which is plain chocolate mixed with sugar. However, Hershey believed another kind of chocolate could become even more popular in the United States: milk chocolate.

The Hershey Chocolate Company is now called the Hershey Company. It grew from Hershey's small company into the leading chocolate-making company in North America!

Making Milk Chocolate

Hershey wasn't the first person to make milk chocolate. Swiss chocolatiers, or chocolate makers, had made a kind of chocolate using milk for years. However, they kept their recipes a secret, so it was up to Hershey to create his own recipe for milk chocolate.

While Hershey didn't invent milk chocolate, he was the first person to make it using fresh milk. It wasn't easy. Hershey didn't learn his recipe from anyone. As one of his employees put it, "Nobody told

Mixing Milk and Chocolate

Before milk chocolate was created, chocolate was made using dried beans from the cacao plant and their **cocoa butter**. Sometimes sugar was added to make sweet chocolate. Then, in the 1860s, a Swiss chocolatier named Daniel Peter first mixed milk into chocolate. A few years later, his neighbor, Henri Nestlé supplied him with **condensed milk** for his chocolates, creating what became the first successful recipe for milk chocolate. In 1904, Nestlé's company bought the rights to Peter's milk chocolate. Nestlé still sells chocolate and many other products today.

Mr. Hershey how to make milk chocolate. He just found out the hard way," which was years of trial and error.

The first Hershey's milk chocolate bar was sold in 1900. Seven years later, Hershey began making and selling what would become one of his most famous treats: a tiny, cone-shaped piece of chocolate known today as a Hershey's Kiss.

Hershey's Kisses are a very famous candy.

Hershey's Chocolate Factory

It took Hershey a few years after he created the first Hershey's milk chocolate bar to perfect his recipe for milk chocolate. He did this at a new chocolate factory he built in Derry Township. Construction began on the factory in 1903, and it was up and running by 1905.

Hershey's factory was different from many others built around this time in American history. Most factories were built in big cities, but Hershey's factory was in the middle of Pennsylvania farm country. However, Hershey knew he was making the right choice. Derry Township was close to ports in New York and Philadelphia, so he could easily get the sugar and cocoa beans he needed. It was also near many dairy farms that could supply him with the fresh milk he needed to make his popular chocolates.

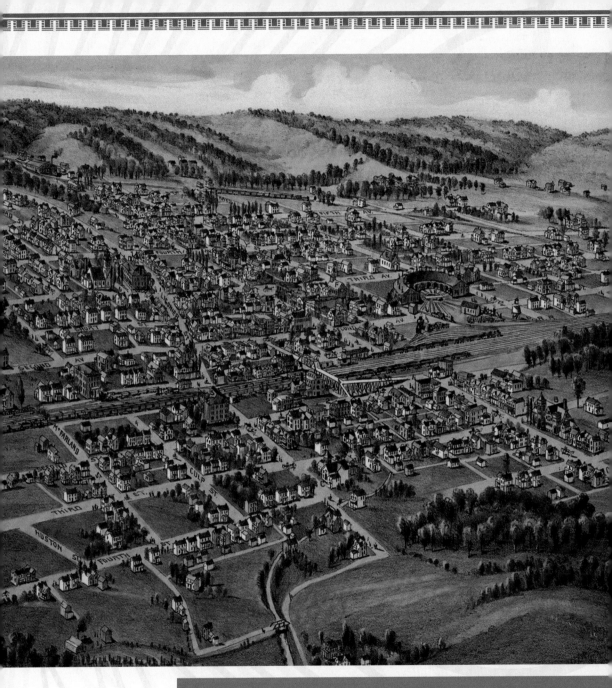

Hershey knew hardworking people lived in Derry Township, and he gave many of them jobs in his new chocolate factory.

Mass Production Changes the Game

At Hershey's chocolate factory, milk chocolate was mass-produced, or made in large amounts using machines. Mass production was an important part of Hershey's success. He might not have been the first person to make milk chocolate, but he was the first person to mass-produce it.

How did Hershey's mass production methods help the chocolate industry grow? By mass-producing chocolate, Hershey made it more quickly and cheaply than if it had been made by hand. This allowed Hershey's chocolate to be sold at a cheaper price and in larger amounts.

Thanks to mass production, Hershey was able to make chocolate that average Americans could enjoy. The Hershey Chocolate Company took what had always been seen as a treat for the rich and made it affordable enough for the masses.

The Industrial Revolution

Hershey's chocolate factory was built during what's sometimes called the Second Industrial Revolution. It's generally accepted that this part of the Industrial Revolution started in the second half of the 19th century and lasted until the start of World War I in 1914. Mass production was an important part of the Industrial Revolution, which was the process of change from making goods by hand in homes and small shops to producing them by machines in factories. Hershey's factory is an example of how the Industrial Revolution affected the American industries.

Hershey applied modern **technology** to the chocolate-making process. This made chocolate an affordable treat for the average American. The first Hershey chocolate bars sold for just five cents!

A Company Town

Hershey didn't just build a factory—he built the community of Hershey around it. Hershey wanted to take care of his workers. He believed they would do better at their jobs if they lived in a good **environment**. With this in mind, he began planning a pleasant community for his workers.

The early community had houses for workers, as well as a building that served as a bank, post office, and place to eat. Other early buildings in Hershey included churches and a store.

Hershey's town also had a **trolley** system that connected it to areas around it. Workers who didn't live in the town used the trolleys to get to and from work. The trolleys also took fresh milk to the chocolate factory.

Hershey grew from a small company town into a major tourist **destination**. One thing has stayed the same, though, and that's the town's focus on chocolate!

Company Towns

During the Industrial Revolution, many people moved from farms to cities to be closer to factories. In some cases, such as that of Hershey's chocolate factory, cities or towns were built around factories if they weren't located in a major **urban** area. These towns are called company towns, and they were most often planned and built by entrepreneurs. Other examples of company towns include Lowell, Massachusetts, which was built around **textile** factories, and Pullman, Illinois, which was constructed for workers in the railroad car industry.

More Than Just Chocolate

Hershey was a great entrepreneur in part because he knew how to take one business and grow it into something greater. What started as a chocolate company and a company town soon grew into a place that attracted visitors from across the country and, eventually, from around the world. People travel to Hershey to take tours of the chocolate factory, and now they also travel there to visit the Hersheypark amusement park.

Hersheypark first opened in 1907 as a public park. However, it grew over time to include a zoo, a swimming pool, and a few rides. Today, it's a major amusement park with huge roller coasters and other rides.

Hersheypark

Hershey created jobs not just in his factory but in the town of Hershey, too. For example, during the **Great Depression**, Hershey employed hundreds of workers through the construction of the Hotel Hershey.

Many Americans were out of work during the Great Depression. Hershey had the Hotel Hershey built to give some of these people jobs. He also wanted to give people a beautiful place to stay when they came to tour his chocolate factory or visit Hersheypark.

Central Hershey, Cuba

In 1916, Hershey bought a sugar mill in Cuba because World War I was making it hard to ship sugar to the United States. Following the model of his company town in Pennsylvania, he built a town around this mill, too. The town of Central Hershey had schools, a baseball diamond, and homes for workers. It also had a railroad to connect the town to other parts of Cuba. Hershey's workers in Cuba also received good health care. However, after Hershey's death, his mill in Cuba was sold. It finally closed in 2003.

Starting a School

Hershey believed a good education was important for training the next generation of workers. His poor education as a child made him determined to give children in Hershey better opportunities.

In 1909, Hershey and his wife, Catherine, established a school for orphaned boys. This school was set up to teach them basic subjects, agricultural topics, and basic skills for future jobs. The next year, the first 10 students started at that school.

Catherine Hershey

Catherine Sweeney was born in Jamestown, New York. She was a hard worker with a warm personality, but she grew up without much money. This seemed to play a part in her desire to help those less fortunate than her. Catherine married Hershey in May 1898. The two never had children, but Catherine worked with her husband to provide many children with a home and a good education. In fact, Hershey said the school for orphans was his wife's idea. Catherine died in 1915 after being sick for many years, and Hershey never remarried.

In 1924, Hershey said, "I wanted to give as many boys as possible real homes, real comforts, education, and training, so they would be useful and happy citizens." Today, Hershey's efforts to provide education and training for children in Hershey are a big part of his **legacy**.

In 1918, Hershey decided to give most of his fortune to the school, which is still in operation today. Now called Milton Hershey School, it's open to both boys and girls. It provides **underserved** children with a free private education as well as free housing and medical care.

Hershey's on the Rise

Hershey's milk chocolate continued to grow in popularity as time went on. His company even created chocolate bars that soldiers were given in their **rations** during World War II. One of these kinds of chocolate bars—Hershey's Tropical Chocolate Bar—was made to stay solid in warm parts of the world where other chocolate bars would melt. In 1971, these chocolate bars went into space! Astronauts took some with them on the Apollo 15 mission to the moon.

Although Hershey died on October 13, 1945, his company continued to grow. In 1963, the company bought the H.B. Reese Candy Company, which was famous for its peanut butter cups. Today, it's believed that the sale of Reese's Peanut Butter Cups makes more than $516 million each year for the Hershey Company.

More than a century after Hershey made his first milk chocolate bar, Hershey bars are still loved today. They're the best-selling chocolate bar in the United States, with around $475 million in yearly sales.

A Lasting Legacy

Hershey wasn't an overnight success. He failed many times before succeeding as an entrepreneur, but his chocolate company created the milk chocolate industry in the United States. It continues to set the industry standard in North America as the continent's most successful chocolate company.

However, Hershey isn't known only for his contributions to the chocolate industry. He's also famous for what he did after bringing milk chocolate to people in the United States. Millions of tourists visit the community of Hershey each year, and Milton Hershey School helps many children in Hershey's hometown.

Milton Hershey used his chocolate fortune to help others and build a successful town. Hershey's company and the town that bears his name continue to grow, keeping his legacy alive long after he made his first chocolate bar.

Hershey made chocolate available to regular Americans, and his company continues to do that on an even larger scale today. No matter how far the Hershey Company reaches, though, its roots will always be in the Pennsylvania community named after its founder.

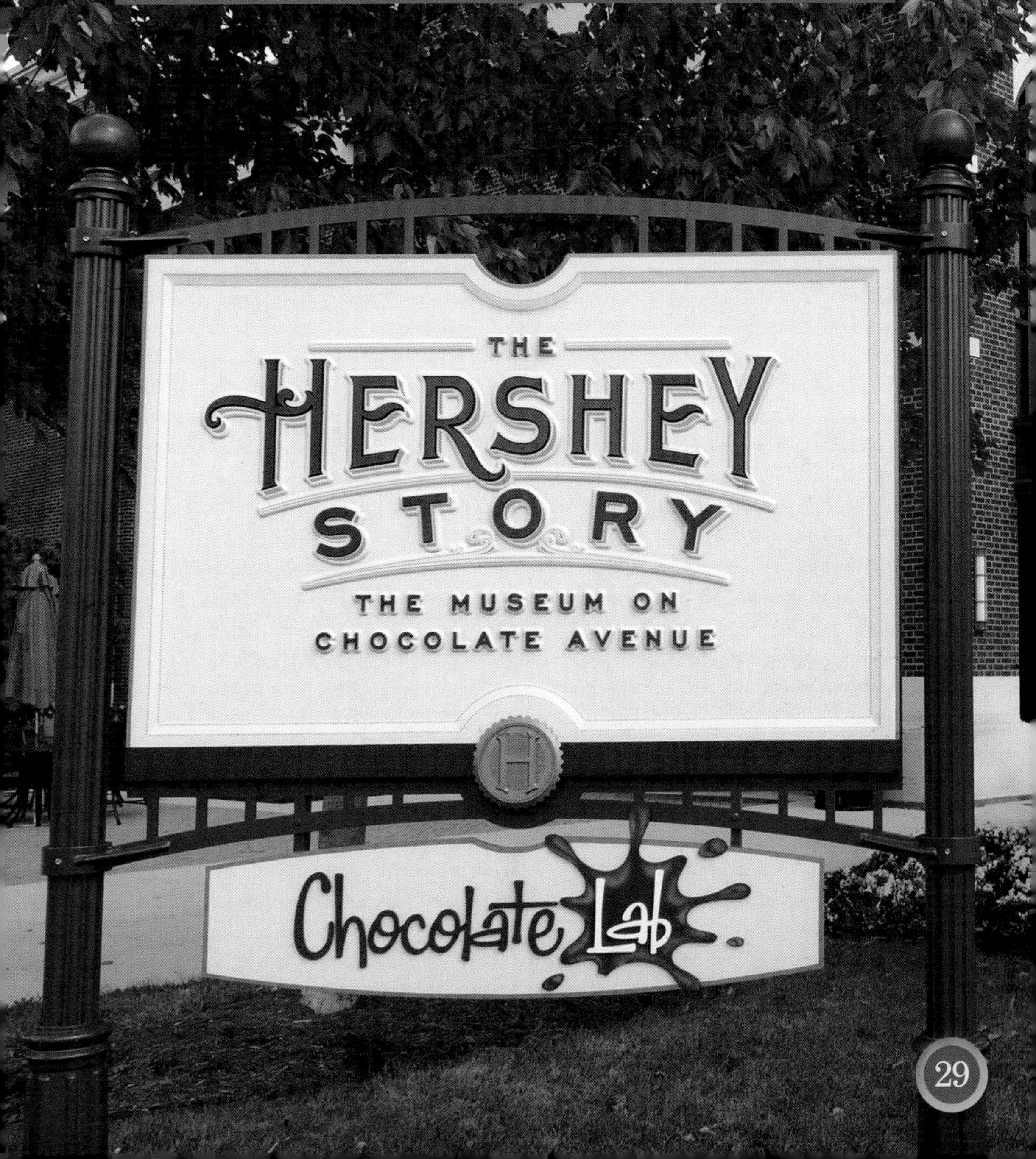

THE
HERSHEY
STORY

THE MUSEUM ON
CHOCOLATE AVENUE

H

Chocolate Lab

A Timeline of Milton Hershey's Life

1857 — Milton Hershey is born in Derry Township, Pennsylvania.

1876 — Hershey moves to Philadelphia to start a candy business.

1893 — Hershey travels to the World's Columbian Exposition in Chicago and buys an entire set of German chocolate-making equipment.

1894 — Hershey establishes the Hershey Chocolate Company.

1896 — Hershey buys a milk-processing plant in Derry Township.

1900 — Hershey sells the Lancaster Caramel Company for $1 million and sells his first milk chocolate bar.

1903 — Construction begins on Hershey's chocolate factory and a community around it in Derry Township.

1907 — The first Hershey's Kiss is sold, and Hersheypark opens.

1909 — Hershey and Catherine start what's now called the Milton Hershey School.

1915 — Catherine Hershey dies.

1916 — Hershey buys a sugar mill in Cuba.

1945 — Milton Hershey dies.

1963 — The Hershey Company purchases the H.B. Reese Candy Company.

Glossary

cocoa butter: A fat that comes from cacao beans.

condensed milk: Canned milk with sugar added and much of the water removed.

destination: A place to which a person is going.

environment: Everything that is around a person.

Great Depression: A period of worldwide economic hardship and unemployment that lasted from 1929 to around 1940.

legacy: Something that comes from someone in the past.

ration: A particular amount of food that is given to a person.

technology: The use of science to solve problems and the tools used to solve those problems.

textile: Woven cloth or fiber.

trolley: A vehicle that is pulled along tracks on the ground by a moving cable or that hangs from a moving cable.

underserved: Not given access to certain important services, such as health and social services.

urban: Relating to a city.

variety: A thing that differs in some way from others of the same general kind, such as different flavors of candy.

Index

Websites

Due to the changing nature of Internet links, PowerKids Press has developed an online list of websites related to the subject of this book. This site is updated regularly. Please use this link to access the list: www.powerkidslinks.com/entre/hers